TWELVE WAYS TO SHARE JESUS WITHOUT SAYING A WORD

RICK MCKINNEY

Table of Contents

Most people who know me would never guess what I'm getting ready to tell you...I'm a very profound introvert! Fifty years in ministry have forced me to learn how to be what I call a "functioning" introvert in social situations but left to my own devices; I would rarely mingle with strangers at a party or talk to anyone on the street. That has always made "witnessing" very difficult for me. Some of the ideas you're about to read have come out of those many years of evangelism frustration. Others I've discovered are just plain fun and even more effective than talking, especially when it comes to strangers.

Many Christians believe that sharing Jesus requires a smooth presentation with lots of memorized Scriptures. Others think you have to draw diagrams on napkins while you talk your way through the plan of salvation. While many people have been led to the foot of the cross using these methods, the truth is that the vast majority of believers don't feel confident enough to witness this way.

Over the years, I have developed, without really meaning to, a lifestyle of evangelism that works even for those of us who are timid about engaging in gospel conversations. This doesn't mean we should never use words to share our faith, but it is to say there are a variety of ways to spread the good news "silently."

The goal, after all, is to impress people with the love of God. That's what the gospel is, the story of God's love for humankind. John's first epistle makes it clear that the progression goes something like this: God loved us, we responded by loving Him and the natural outcome of that relationship is that we love others. In other words: Love God, Love People. Jesus said that our love for our fellow man is how people will know we are His. And for most folks, love is best illustrated not through words but through visible actions. Those actions don't require any words, but they can make a definite impact on those who are the recipients of "silent evangelism." Here are a few ideas on how to share the gospel without saying a word... or at least not many.

SIGN LANGUAGE

One of my very favorite ways to let people know God loves them is with big, bold signs. I first did this many years ago when we lived close to an Interstate entrance ramp. I made signs with posterboard and wide markers that said things like "Smile, God Loves You," or "Jesus Loves Everyone." Then I'd go out to the entrance ramp early in the morning as people were getting on the Interstate to go to work. Think about it. Most folks are a little sleepy; work and have lots on their minds as they start their day. They reluctantly round the corner to merge onto the highway and a guy is standing there with a sign that says, "Jesus is Thinking About You!"

Although this may push you out of your comfort zone a bit, it is a way to get many "impressions" quickly. On any given day I might have had 50-100 cars pass by me in an hour or so. Most of those cars had one or two people headed off to work. Many of them waved, some beeped their horns and yes, a few looked the other way. But without speaking a word, at least 100 people knew God cared.

My guess is that many of them had a better day at work, smiled a little more and most importantly, for the next few moments as they drove to work, contemplated their relationship with God.

COVERT OPERATION

I read about this in a book on evangelism many years ago and have since tried it several times. Not everyone has the nerve to do it. Still, I think as long as your heart is right and you use printed materials that are tasteful and encouraging, no one will be offended, and some may even be prompted to think about their relationship with God for the first time in a long time.

While we're talking about printed materials, let's discuss what kinds of things we're talking about. Keep it positive, encouraging and focused on God's love. There is a time and place to speak about judgment and wrath, but this kind of situation is not it. There's nothing worse than picking up a gospel tract that shouts in bold letters, "You're Going to Hell." I'm *not* going to hell and that offends me! Imagine how someone else may feel who isn't sure about their eternal destination. Remember, the aim of this kind of sharing is to let discouraged, confused and disenfranchised people know that there is a God who loves them and wants to include them in His family. Also, I'd stay away from flyers about church events. That could cause the church to get a reputation that's a bit negative.

Once you've found the perfect literature to leave behind, visit a store with a wide variety of products. Insert your tracts in magazines/books, in the pocket of a shirt or blouse, or even in a small appliance box that isn't sealed. Don't destroy any property or damage anything. Don't put your name or church name on the tract. That diminishes the chances that you'll offend a customer or, worse, the store's management. In case someone does ask you to stop…stop. Your testimony is more important, so apologize if you've offended anyone and leave. It's OK. The ones you left will reach the right people. Don't visit the same store over and over. Go to different places, even places when you're traveling. I have to admit that this is great fun in addition to being a great witness.

BRIGHTEN THE CORNER

Here's one that everyone can do! Most everyone has access to a computer and printer these days. I encourage you to use this method instead of a marker or something that looks less than professional. God deserves our best efforts and representation, so go the extra mile on this one and it will be welcomed by most.

Many stores, restaurants and coffee shops have bulletin boards where patrons can post a small poster about an upcoming event or an announcement. You'll be much more likely to receive permission if it's a place where you are recognized as a frequent customer and if your sign looks bright and encouraging.

Design a colorful, cheerful sign that brings a smile to people's faces and points them to Jesus. Don't just use text but add some colorful pictures as well. Maybe even a pleasant border that matches the season. Make it no larger than 8.5X11. Here's an example of one I made up in about 5 minutes.

I made two things to bloom...
Flowers...
And You!

Bloom where you're planted today!
And remember...I love you.
                                    -Jesus

You can make six or eight of these up in no time at all. I suggest switching them out at the locations every two months or so. If you do a nice job, many places will look forward to you bringing new posters and will welcome your uplifting addition to the bulletin board.

EAT, DRINK AND BE...HELPFUL

Few things are as appealing as cold water when you're thirsty or a candy bar when you need a snack. This is one of the easiest ways to leave a good impression and to share Jesus without saying a word.

I like to give away water during warm months at local parks and places where people walk, run or exercise. If they exercise regularly, they may have their own water or other drink, but many will welcome your gesture of kindness. A couple of tricks make this one more successful, and you can experiment to see what works best for you.

You can buy mailing labels at your local office supply or big box store. Labels that are approximately 3" X 5" work well with water bottles. Print them off on your printer and have them ready. Don't apply them to the bottles too soon, especially if you're going to put them on ice or submerge them in ice water. The ink will run, and the label will peel off. This will work best if you have a partner accompanying you. They can be in charge of the labels. Walk around the park with a small cooler containing your cold waters. As you approach someone to offer them water, wipe the cold bottle off and attach the label just before handing it to them. Your label should say something like, "This water is a gift to remind you that God loves you." If that's a little too "preachy" for you, try this humorous label: "God told me you might be thirsty."

Just be sensitive, kind and greet people with a smile. You'll be surprised how appreciative people will be when you show them a little love.

Candy bars can be a little tricky these days because of nut allergies. Try to find candy or snacks with no nuts, or at least have an alternative snack (prepackaged) with no nuts. Attach a catchy label and pass them out. This works at any event where there are people. People are pretty protective of their children these days, so don't approach them with candy unless the parent is present. Ask the parent if the child can have candy first. Of course, adults like candy bars and snacks too, so don't leave them out. Remember, it's not about the water or candy. It's about showing the love of God to others in tangible ways.

ARE YOU PACKIN'?

Years ago, I kept hearing the phrase "Random Acts of Kindness." I liked the idea but felt the phrase didn't convey what believers should do regarding sharing their faith. First, our acts of kindness shouldn't be random, but we should plan every day to share Jesus in some way…that very day. Second, we aren't just kind because we're good people but because we are Christians. So, I coined the phrase "Planned Acts of Christian Kindness," P.A.C.K. for short.

I ordered some business cards from an online company (they are very reasonably priced and 100 cards will last a long time). This is what they looked like:

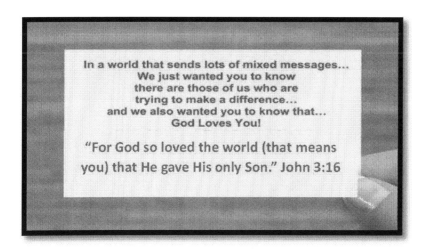

In a world that sends lots of mixed messages...
We just wanted you to know
there are those of us who are
trying to make a difference...
and we also wanted you to know that...
God Loves You!

"For God so loved the world (that means you) that He gave His only Son." John 3:16

Then the fun begins. Pull into your favorite coffee shop drive-thru. After you pay for your own coffee, tell the person at the window that you'd like to pay for the person's coffee behind you. Just ask them to give them the P.A.C.K card when they tell them their order is paid for. It also works for food drive-thrus, although that can get more expensive.

Only your imagination will limit the places you can use a P.A.C.K. card. You can paper clip a one-dollar bill to the card and drop it (on purpose) in a grocery store aisle or put it in the toy section of a department store where a child will find it.

You can buy a few things you know a senior adult could use, put them in a basket and drop in a P.A.C.K. card. Put it on their front porch and ring the bell, and RUN! Seeing people's reactions when they are blessed is so much fun. But don't let them know it was you. That will take the focus off of Jesus.

BROWN BAGGIN' IT

We tried this a few years ago and it works wonderfully! Get a few brown paper bags and fill them with breakfast-type items. We used a piece of fruit, a granola bar, a small, sealed, chilled orange juice, and a Twinkie® or something similar. Don't forget to drop in a P.A.C.K. card or even a handwritten note with something like: "Have a great day! Hope this helps you get off to a great start. And remember, God loves you."

Then head out to an intersection in your town with a traffic light. Go at the time when people are headed off to work for the day. Dress casually but neatly and when the light turns red, go up to the window of a stopped car and offer them a bag. If you're comfortable sharing a greeting, fine. If not, just hand them the bag.

Have your children or a Sunday School class decorate the bags with crayons or markers for an extra kick.

BEING SOCIABLE

We have all experienced the power of social media. The statistics detailing how much time the average person spends on social media platforms like Facebook®, Twitter® and Instagram® are astounding. Without saying a word, we know details about other people's lives that we would have had no way of knowing just a few years ago. For all the negative things that could be said about these platforms, the truth is that they can also have a huge positive influence as well.

For example, my wife posts several memes each morning containing Scripture verses. They are always encouraging and point the readers to Christ. Here's an example:

BE ON GUARD.
Stand firm in the faith.
BE COURAGEOUS.
Be strong.

1 CORINTHIANS 16:13 NLT

K-LOVE

If you're creative, you can create your own. Otherwise, several websites allow you to receive new ones daily through email. It's OK to copy and paste them on your feed.

My wife also posts something daily called "My Hymn for the Day." She has almost 1000 followers who get the historical background of a hymn each morning, along with the words of the hymn. What a great way to share Jesus without saying a word or singing a note.

I sometimes like to post Christian music. Make sure it's good quality and is something your friends will enjoy. If you know how to put up a link to a YouTube® video, that's all you need to do. You can comment if you like. Something like, "I hope you'll listen to this song. It's well worth a few minutes of your time."

Another idea is to repost quotes by well-known Christians or retweet quotes from others on Twitter. Social media is still a wide-open mission field as long as you are tactful and pleasant. Remember that consistency in your posts is essential. Don't post about Jesus one day and rant and curse the next. That will neutralize any effect your good posts have.

SNAIL MAIL

There's nothing like going to the mailbox and finding an envelope that's hand addressed with a return address you recognize. Most of us have stopped sending hand-written notes through the United States Postal Service in this digital age. We text, email, send Facebook® messages and use a phone for talking, but we just don't write much.

Think of some of your friends or family who don't have a relationship with Christ. What do they need? Maybe they need something picked up at the grocery or a ride somewhere. Perhaps they would appreciate an invitation to have coffee or a meal. Use a hand-written note to offer help. Be pleasant, upbeat and present the offer as something you'd like to do, as opposed to something they need. They may not accept the offer the first time, but if not, offer again in a few weeks. If you take them for coffee or a meal, you may have to talk, but it'll probably be best to let them do most of the talking anyway.

Lonely folks like to tell you about themselves and even ask for advice. That's a great start.

DO IT BY THE YARD

You probably have an old yard sign lying around somewhere. Maybe it's from a past political election, school event, or yard sale. You can repurpose it by painting over the sign (it may take a couple of coats) and then neatly printing a message that points to Christ. Don't be hateful or graphic.

No threats of hell. Keep it positive with something like, "I prayed for my neighbors today." If you use that one, make sure to pray for your neighbors.

HE IS MY
REFUGE
AND MY
FORTRESS
MY GOD
IN WHOM I TRUST

If you really want to make it attractive, you can design something on your computer and have a local print shop print it large enough to cover the yard sign. When your neighbors know you are a person of faith, they will likely come to you when they need help or wise counsel,. Here are a couple of ideas:

WEAR IT...SHARE IT

Here's one that everyone can do. Wear clothing (t-shirts, sweatshirts, hats) proclaiming your faith in Christ. No spoken words are needed. Again, not one with a gory picture of Jesus on the cross with blood dripping down from His hands. We know that's the reality, but it's off-putting until a person is ready to receive that part of the message. The reason He died was because of love. Share His love. It could even be a question. For example, "Did you know Jesus loves you?" Of course, you might have to say something if given the opportunity.

We wear Christian clothing a lot! Sometimes it gets responses from other believers and that's great, but we really want non-Christians to see the message and start thinking positively about Jesus.

BOOK IT!

Of course, you might expect an author to say this, but giving someone the right book is sometimes just the thing to get them thinking about God, Jesus and eternity. There are many readers out there (61% of Americans say they read at least one book last year). They may not read a Bible if you give them one, but they might read an interesting book written from a Christian perspective. There are thousands of Christian books including Christian fiction, romance, science fiction, biographies and even mysteries.

Everyone likes gifts and giving a book might just be the right approach for the friend who wants to read more than talk.

TAKE UP YOUR CROSS

OK, this will be the one that you may think, "I'd never do that." But as someone very wise once said, "Never say never!"

Many years ago, I followed in the footsteps of one of my heroes and made a giant wooden cross. I put a small wheel on the back and convinced some of my congregation to join me in carrying the cross for 45 miles over three days. It was amazing! Years later, I did the same thing with another congregation in a different location. One day I carried the cross to the Post Office and passed out gospel tracts. A couple of years later, we made four crosses and carried them from four different locations, met at Fountain Square in Cincinnati and had a huge rally.

It's a bold witness, not for the faint of heart. But if you want to make a big statement, this may be for you. You don't have to say a word...because the cross says it all.

FINAL THOUGHTS

I want to say this loud and clear: We need to unapologetically proclaim our faith in Christ. We not only have a responsibility to do this as His ambassadors but also the privilege to share the good news that saved us. However, we also must remember that we live in a different world than 50 years ago. The heavy-handed evangelistic techniques that seemed to get results then are hard to get away with today.

Although we must be clear about Jesus' sacrificial death on the cross and the result of rejecting the offer of forgiveness, we must also be loving, kind and gentle in our approach with most people. Wordless evangelism isn't the complete answer to sharing the gospel, but it can open doors and prompt questions that may lead to spoken gospel conversations.

I encourage you to take these ideas and put them into practice. Perhaps you could commit to trying one each week for the next twelve weeks. Refine the ideas to fit your lifestyle, but at least do something to begin the practice of living your faith out loud, even if you never say a word.

Made in the USA
Middletown, DE
19 June 2023

32372565R00018